DELEGATION

The saying is trustworthy: If anyone aspires to the
office of overseer, he desires a noble task.
1 Timothy 3:1
English Standard Version

DELEGATION

The Most Rewarding, Frustrating . . .
Awesome Part of Running Your Business

DAVE RAMSEY

RAMSEY
P R E S S

Editorial: Jackie Quinn

Cover Design: Weylon Smith and Chris Carrico

Interior Design: PerfecType, Nashville, TN

ISBN: 978-1-942121-76-3

Printed in the United States of America

22 23 24 25 26 POL 5 4 3 2 1

INTRODUCTION

Run. Run. Run. Every day, from the minute you roll out of bed in the morning to the minute you collapse back in bed at night, it feels like you're running a race. A demanding, exhausting, unforgiving race. But . . . it's a race you've chosen.

Or so you thought.

You wanted to be an entrepreneur, to have your own company and contribute to the world in your own unique way. So you built a business. And with it came the title CEO: chief executive officer. It had a nice ring to it.

Then your business grew. And your CEO title grew too: chief everything officer. Before you knew it, you were wearing a fifty-pound firefighter suit underneath your business casual attire and racing from small campfires to full-fledged infernos. All. Day. Long.

And that's not counting all the fires that seemed to flare up after hours. You cringe just thinking about all the times you've sat on the sidelines at your kids' sports events or in the audience at their school music programs, only half tuned in to the shots made or the solos sung because you're on your phone catching up on Mayday emails you couldn't get to during the day. And you can't even bring yourself to think about how many times you've had to cancel date nights with your spouse because you needed to work late.

Now you're just plain tired, and you're not sure how much longer you can run. Or if you even want to. But you keep gutting it out and telling yourself *you've come too far to only come this far.* You keep holding on to the hope that there's got to be a better, more sustainable way.

As a young entrepreneur, I found myself caught between exhaustion and hope too. When I was at this stage in building my business, I was delivering books out of the trunk of my car. I was helping to unload boxes off the truck with the rest of the team after we got done doing a live event. Nobody on the team had just one job. No one ever said, "That's not in my job description," because we all had to do everything. I'd get home after work and fall on the couch exhausted, and my wife, Sharon, would ask, "What did you do today?" And I'd say, "I have no freaking idea!" and sink even further into the couch, like the weight of the entire world was on me.

You see, when you're running a small business, doing everything *is* your job description. You're just trying to make payroll on Friday. You're watching cash flow like a hawk. Your time-management skills aren't great at this stage because you just run from one on-fire thing to the next. Deep down you know you need help, and you even make feeble attempts at delegating. But in the end, you create more of a mess, and you conclude that it's just easier to do things yourself.

That was me. I was building Ramsey Solutions, trying to grow my team from seven to twenty team members but still running in all the lanes and doing all the things. I told myself, *It's because I care so much* and *No one cares as much as I do*. But something was off. Something was broken.

Turns out . . . I sucked at delegation!

Or so I thought.

What I realized is that I really wasn't that far off at all. I just needed to get really clear on what delegation is and isn't. Then I could better develop a process to do handoffs well. Once I got that figured out, I could intentionally and strategically stop doing and being all the things and start empowering my team to carry more of the weight so we could scale. It's made all the difference.

Maybe this is you right now. You've got your hands and head in all the things, and you're teetering on the edge of burnout. You know something needs to change to get to the next level in your business, but you don't know how to effectively do the handoffs that will get you there. Or you might just be too scared to hand something off at all because you've always been the person who's done the thing your business is built on.

Consider this book your road map. In the pages ahead, I'll break down the concept of delegation and show you how to strategically apply it to your company's growth. You'll learn when and how to intentionally delegate and, in turn, develop healthy expectations and boundaries for yourself and your team. But I want to warn you: once you start delegating, you'll wonder how you ever lived and worked without it!

Are you ready? Let's do this!

WHAT DELEGATION IS

The best analogy I can give to show you what delegation is starts with a story about the Ramsey kids as teenagers.

When Denise, Rachel, and Daniel hit their teenage years, Sharon and I discovered that the single greatest thing they wanted was to be treated like adults. Of course, my constant response to this was, "Then freaking act like an adult!" Believe me, I had the same goal too: for them to become adults so that someday they'd leave. Having a thirty-year-old living in my basement was never part of my plan. But like every teenager, they struggled some days to reach the goal because in their fifteen-year-old bodies also lived a four-year-old and a thirty-four-year-old. And depending on the day or the circumstance, Sharon and I had no idea which one was going to come out. It was like they had multiple personalities. (If you're a parent of a teen, you know what I'm talking about.)

To help the three of them navigate their teen emotions, decision-making, and the freedoms they said they wanted, I came up with "the rope" teaching metaphor. The rope was a great way for them to visualize the levels of trust they could build with us and other adults. I told them that as their dad, I had an invisible rope attached to them. With every trustworthy thing they did, I would lengthen the rope. That meant if they were actually going where they said they were going and doing what they said they were doing, I lengthened the rope. That also meant if they lied about anything or chose to do what their friends said and not what their parents said, I shortened the rope.

For example, if we agreed they could go to a movie and that I'd pick them up outside of the theater when it was over, but then they called after the movie to tell me they'd decided to go to McDonald's instead . . . *wrong answer*. That's not what we had agreed to. That busted the trust. The rope got shorter, and Humpty Dumpty was harder to put back together again.

Now, if they were at a party and I got a call from them that they needed me to come get them because the host parents had suddenly left and adult beverages and left-handed cigarettes had appeared on the scene, then I was there as quick as I could get there. You know what a phone call like that got them? Lots of rope. Lots of freedom. Because it proved their ability to make good decisions in tough situations. And with every good decision came more rope and more opportunities to make more good decisions.

That's how the rope worked. When they messed up, the rope was shorter, and I watched them more closely. But the better choices they made, the further I lengthened the rope and let them go on their own.

So when our oldest child, Denise, got ready to go off to college, we held a special family dinner—fancy, like in the actual dining room with china dishes and cloth napkins. We wanted to celebrate her accomplishments and her adventures ahead. Rachel, the middle child, dramatically describes it more like a funeral wake where we cried and lamented about Denise as if she wasn't there. Let's just say, it was definitely a night of mixed emotions.

After dinner, we gathered in the rec room to give a special gift to Denise. A few days before, I had stopped by the local craft store and bought some white drapery rope and some colored ribbon. I coiled the rope and tied it with the different colors of ribbon: a purple ribbon to represent her spiritual walk, a red ribbon to represent her academics, a white ribbon to represent her purity, a yellow ribbon to represent the safe and stable foundation she'd always have at home, and an orange ribbon for the University of Tennessee, where she'd be attending (Go Vols!).

I gave Denise the rope and told her how proud we were of the mature young woman of God she had become. I reminded her that because of the decisions she had made and how she had chosen to live her life, she had earned our trust. She had become *trustworthy*. We had every confidence she was capable of continuing to making good decisions for her life even though she was moving several hundred miles away. We were entrusting the rope to her because we no longer needed to hold on. We had faith that she would step into all God had for her. It was a powerful rite-of-passage moment that made all our eyes leak.

A couple of months after moving her in at UT, we traveled back to Knoxville to attend a football game and visit Denise. We went to her dorm room, and there, hanging on the bedpost, was the rope. I couldn't believe it. I thought for sure that thing would have been buried at the bottom of a box and stuffed in the back of the closet.

"What's up with the rope?" I asked Denise. She said, "Oh, Dad, the rope is legendary! Girls come from three dorms over to hear the story of the rope." Wow.

It sounds crazy that a silly rope would have that much impact. But really, it's not crazy at all. The rope signified years of training, repetition, mistakes, growth, and earned trust. It represented integrity and competency built over time. Ultimately, it represented the delegation of responsibility to someone who was *ready*.

Now, I realize you're dealing with adults in your company, not teenagers (at least I hope so). But the metaphor still works. Delegation is the lengthening of the rope. It's how you confidently build your team. It's how you grow quality team members and scale. It's how you avoid dysfunction and cultivate integrity and competency across your team. But before we get too deep on the *how*, let's finish the *what* and get really clear about what delegation *isn't*.

WHAT DELEGATION ISN'T

Have you ever been accused of, or accused yourself of, being a micro-manager? Like I mentioned before, I felt like I sucked at delegation because it made me feel like a control freak. But I finally realized that's where many of us leaders get the concept of the rope confused. Letting the rope out and pulling the rope in is *not* controlling or micromanaging. So many of us leaders are so scared to be perceived that way that we go to the extreme ends of the spectrum. We either grip the rope too tightly and never let it go, or we throw the entire rope at the team member all at once—and then wonder why they didn't do a good job!

Delegation is *not* a blind handoff. It's not taking a product or process you as the leader have developed over time—with excellence and high expectations—and then blindly handing it off to some-one on your team while you stand on the sidelines with your fingers crossed, hoping they might replicate the process with the same excel-lence and high expectations. That's not delegation. That's stupid.

Delegation is a well-thought-out, step-by-step process. It's inten-tionally shifting the responsibility for particular functions, tasks, or decisions from one person on your team to another person who's been *properly trained* and is *ready*. It's lengthening and shortening the rope while that person learns. It's not blindly handing off something just to get it done. Only a fool would do that.

For example, I'm not giving the keys to my brand-new Porsche to someone who's never had a driving lesson. And I'm sure as heck not letting someone I just met in the checkout aisle at the grocery store come to my house and babysit my baby while I leave for the day! It's impossible to overmanage a person who's new to the team or new to a role. After all, they're still figuring out where the bathrooms are and how to navigate the traffic patterns to and from work.

At the same time, you *can* overmanage someone who's grown on the job and proven their integrity and competency in a role. *That* is micromanaging, not delegation. It's important to make the distinction.

For instance, if you're eighty-three years old and your son is sixty-seven, it's time to let go and turn the company over. In fact, you're twenty years late! By this time, you should have turned the company over or fired your son and brought in more competent leaders. The idea that you're just going to wait and wait until it's convenient for you isn't a good succession plan in family business—or any business for that matter. This is micromanaging at its worst.

Micromanagers are control freaks who don't have the maturity to allow themselves to trust in a team member's competency and integrity. Micromanagers are like an interfering mother-in-law after a couple's been married ten years. You know the one—she's looking down her nose and still telling the husband and wife how to make dinner, run their household, and be better parents.

Delegation requires maturity from both the leader and the team member, but the leader *must* lead this. The leader needs to be mature enough to set the tone through their own integrity, work ethic, and speed. In other words, leader, don't delegate and then go play golf! Be mature and discerning enough to give the team member room to learn and grow. And then when the team member is ready, be mature and discerning enough to get out of the way and give them room to run.

Resisting a blind handoff isn't micromanaging—it's wise. Making sure excellence and expectations remain intact is not being a control freak—it's wise. Using discernment to lengthen and shorten the rope is wise. When delegation is done maturely and intentionally, only a fool *wouldn't* delegate.

WHY DELEGATE?

Delegation is a critical strategy for growth. In order for you to grow your capacity, expand your footprint, and serve more people, you need someone else to help you do more work than you can do by yourself. It's that simple. The only reason you would ever hire or promote someone is to be able to delegate to them. Yet delegation is one of the most misunderstood—and even abused—areas of leadership.

Throughout my thirty years of coaching entrepreneurs and business leaders (at Ramsey Solutions we call them EntreLeaders), I've found that most turn to delegation out of desperation. They feel overwhelmed by their growing workload, so they hire or promote people to take the pressure off themselves. On the surface, it seems strategic and growth-minded, but really, it's an emotional reaction to a situation that feels out of control. And once the team member gets in their new seat, the leader has no plan for how and when to turn that person loose to do what they're supposed to do. This creates another layer of confusion and chaos—times two! In the end, what's meant to boost growth actually blocks growth. It's oxymoronic. And it's what separates a boss from being a true leader.

Leaders have a plan and a growth strategy for their company and their people. As a young business owner, you might be tempted to hire people quickly and have them carry out tasks and goals that you don't want to fool with. You might expect people to read your mind and do things you don't like to do. But when you delegate to someone improperly, you make a huge mess and add more drama to your life than you had before. However, when you properly plan and prepare your organization's culture first, delegation will bring peace and joy to your work—and ultimately your life.

Think of it this way: Leaders are the conductors in the front of the train, setting the path, the process, and the pace. Leaders say to their teams, "Here's where we're going, why we're going, and how fast we're going. This train's leaving on Monday at 8:00 a.m., so it's up to you—you can run beside, fall behind, or miss the train altogether . . . *or* you can climb on board."

When team members choose to get on board, leaders outline what each person will be doing. At Ramsey Solutions, we call this the team member's Key Results Area, or KRA. We'll discuss this further in the How to Delegate section of the book, but for now, understand that a KRA specifically outlines the work each team member is responsible for and what success looks like in their role. The KRA is designed to cover tasks that the leader has strategically determined to delegate to the team member. This gives the team member a clear way of seeing not just how their role supports the leader's work but how it contributes to the greater vision of the company. It also gives the leader the space they need to get out of the weeds and work less tactically and more strategically.

All of this is in huge contrast to a micromanaging boss and their employees. Bosses boss from behind. For example, instead of a conductor on a train, picture a trail boss herding cattle. With a cattle prod and whip, the trail boss tries to push the unruly cattle forward. The cattle are frustrated and don't have a clue where they're going or why, but they get poked, whipped, yelled at, and forced forward anyway. The trail boss is frustrated because the whole herd's speed is dictated by the lowest common denominator plodding along in the back.

Leaders delegate. Bosses micromanage. Leaders pull. Bosses push. Leaders create opportunities for team members to come alongside and play a role as a part of a larger vision. Bosses create frustration and force team members toward an unclear goal. It seems so clear which is the better approach. So why would leaders not delegate?

WHY LEADERS DON'T DELEGATE

Every leader wants to grow their business. But often, so much of their identity is placed in their work that they struggle to let go. And even when they do get past their fears of letting go and actually decide to delegate, there are still two main challenges that can keep many leaders stuck:

1.   They've hired the wrong people (and kept them!).
2.   They haven't properly trained the people they do have (because they're control freaks!).

There's just no other way around it—in order to delegate well, you've got to build a team you can release control to.

Now, this book is a Quick Read about delegation, not the actual hiring process. If you're in that stage of growth, then the Ramsey EntreLeadership team has all kinds of resources for you that break down in detail how to hire and build a team successfully. (Check out *12 Components to a Good Hire* at ramseysolutions.com/delegation.)

As a quick drive-by, I'll just highlight a few key pieces to setting the stage for delegation:

- Hire and train thoroughbreds (not donkeys).
- Compensate team members properly.
- Build unity and loyalty among your team.
- Recognize team members' achievements.

This part of the process can be lengthy, but it's critical *and* rewarding. It takes time to fill your stable full of thoroughbreds. But you can only delegate to thoroughbreds. You cannot delegate to donkeys. A donkey has never won the Kentucky Derby. I repeat: you cannot delegate to donkeys. So take the time to hire and properly train your team first. This is the foundation for creating a delegable environment.

If you have a great hiring process and a great culture in place, it still takes time for a new team member to learn your company's core values and operating principles. New team members must not only have the talent to do the task, but they must also do it within your culture. As much as the start-up phenomena has led us to believe that rushing to grow as fast as possible is the way to success, the idea that you can plug-and-play talent into your company often doesn't work. You can't just add water, microwave for a few minutes, and have an instant leader you can delegate to.

At Ramsey, we hire rock stars, but it still takes most people about a year to really find their footing and be effective in our culture. Our chief marketing officer is one of the smartest women I've ever met in my life. She's got a marketing mind like a trap, and she's unbelievably efficient. She was formerly the CMO at a huge company. Our chief financial officer is another mastermind. Before coming to Ramsey, he was the CFO for the Nashville Predators—again, no small gig. Both of them are sharp as tacks, but even with all their experience and talent, I didn't just toss them the keys, say "good luck," and walk away. I was a part of every decision they made at first, lengthening the rope bit by bit until they were able to finish my sentences. It took both of them about a year to adapt to the way we do things at Ramsey. Once they did, then they could fully bring their brilliance to their work, and in turn, lift our company by building their marketing and finance teams in the same way.

WHEN TO DELEGATE

So far, we've covered what delegation is and isn't and why leaders should or shouldn't delegate. But the question remains: When do you know it's time to delegate? When are you sure you can make the handoff to a team member and they're going to handle customer relationships well? When will you know they can handle your brand and your reputation in the marketplace?

When a team member consistently demonstrates these two critical qualities, you can trust them enough to delegate to them: *integrity* and *competency*. If you get nothing else from this book, get this! Circle it and put stars all around it:

> **In order for a leader to delegate, they**
> **have to completely trust in the team**
> **member's *integrity* and *competency*.**

Integrity

The word *integrity* comes from the root word *integer*. An integer is any whole number not broken into fractions. The same is true with life. A life that isn't broken into fractions is a whole life. In his book

Integrity, my friend Dr. Henry Cloud explains that a life of integrity is a life lived in wholeness or completeness. How does that play out at the office? If a team member isn't generally the same person at work as they are outside of work, they're living a fractured life. If their actions are inconsistent in different settings, then they're lacking integrity and can't be trusted. You can only delegate important tasks to someone to the degree that you can trust their integrity.

If one of my team members lies, steals, or cheats, I instantly fire them. Period. I have zero tolerance for these things. If someone on our team has an adulterous affair, they don't get to stay on the team. Their wholeness is broken. If their spouse can't trust them, I can't trust them either. Can they be redeemed? Absolutely. Can they recover? Absolutely. Will I help them get the resources and counseling they need so they can recover? Absolutely. But not while they're working at Ramsey Solutions. I don't want to be looking over my shoulder the whole time they're on the team, wondering what else is going on.

You also need to see consistency in a team member's integrity over time. Don't give important tasks to unproven people. That only leads to drama and trouble. Often a new team member will come in and hit a big home run, making them the new team favorite. But a one-hit wonder doesn't necessarily prove wholeness. Sure, they have talent in one area, but you need to be able to observe consistency in their work and their life before you can delegate to them.

For example, we've all seen famous celebrities crash for one reason or another. We celebrate that they're talented in one area of their life, so we often assume they're awesome in all areas of their life. We think if they score acrobatic touchdowns or give chart-topping musical performances, they must also be amazing husbands and wives and parents. But you can't "sort of" crash. A crash is evidence that there's a fracture between talent and character. Think of it this way: You can't put two drops of poison in a glass of water and say, "Just don't drink the top part." Integrity demands consistency. And consistency demands diligence.

To maintain a consistently high level of integrity, a team member must have diligence to keep it there. Not only did they once hit a home run, but they also show up and do batting practice every freaking day so they can continue to hit home runs. Anyone who wants to win pays a price: diligence.

Gary Player is a successful professional golfer from South Africa. He was the third man ever to win the four major tournaments that make up golf's distinguished Grand Slam.[1] There's an old story passed among golfers of Gary practicing his drive. On one particular shot, he took a swing and jacked the ball four hundred yards. A spectator in the gallery said, "Man, I'd give anything to hit a ball like that." Gary responded, "No you wouldn't. You wouldn't stand out here and hit two thousand balls until your hands bleed from the broken blisters. You wouldn't then tape your hands and hit more balls. And you wouldn't wake up the next morning, ice your sore and swollen hands for forty-five minutes, then hit another two thousand balls. You wouldn't do that over and over again to drive the ball the way I do."

Let's just say, there's a reason Gary's often quoted for saying: "The harder you work, the luckier you get."[2] Sure, Gary has talent, but he wouldn't have been consistently successful over his career without diligence. It's the price you pay if you want to win.

In his book *Outliers,* Malcolm Gladwell says that practicing ten thousand hours is the "magic number of greatness." If you want to be world-class in any given field, it takes ten thousand hours of practice. You can be naturally gifted as a cellist, but if you want to be world-class, it takes ten thousand hours. If you want to be a household name at whatever "your thing" is, it takes ten thousand hours. You want to be Brad Paisley or Keith Urban on guitar? Work like a maniac. Play the guitar all the time. Write songs and write more songs. My friend Michael W. Smith has written over four thousand songs. He's had thirty-five number one hits. He's earned three Grammys, forty-five Dove Awards and an American Music Award, making him one of the most prolific artists in contemporary Christian music.[3] He's been consistent and diligent to do the work, and it's made all the difference.

Having consistency and diligence is what separates hobbyists from pros. It's what builds and sustains integrity. And it's what grows your team members' capacity to take on more.

Competency

Merriam-Webster defines competency as a "possession of sufficient knowledge or skill." At Ramsey, it means more than that. It's a given that a team member would have sufficient knowledge and skill in the thing we hired them for, or we wouldn't have hired them in the first place! As a part of our hiring process, we give candidates tests to ensure they have the knowledge or skill necessary for writing, editing, designing, coding, marketing, etc. If they don't pass, they don't get the job.

But that's just part of the competency equation. More than having the hard skills, we also evaluate a team member's soft skills—*how* they demonstrate their knowledge and skill. In his book *The Ideal Team Player*, leadership expert Patrick Lencioni describes this with three essential virtues: humble, hungry, and smart. Is the team member humble, adaptable, and open to feedback? Do they know their limitations and when to ask for help? Are they hungry and motivated to do the work with excellence? Will they go above and beyond when necessary? Are they people-smart? Are they conscientious to consider the feelings and communication styles of others? Are they courageous enough to bring you bad news? In other words, there's an important character component to competency that *must* be considered when evaluating a team member's potential to take on more responsibility.

For example, it's one thing for a live event coordinator to help produce and sell eight thousand tickets for a live event. It's another thing to make sure the attendees had an amazing experience. And it's still another thing to make sure the arena staff had a good experience. If there was blatant disregard or miscommunication with the behind-the-scenes crew or they were mistreated in any way at the expense of creating an awesome event, then that's not a successful event at all. That's not humble, hungry, or smart. And it's definitely not complete competency! Getting the job done is not the same as getting the job done with character and excellence.

Dr. Cloud explains character as "the ability to meet the demands of reality." You can't have competency without a demonstration of character. And when all these things come together—when you can consistently observe and measure a team member's competency, integrity, diligence, and character in action—*then* you know they're ready for more. This is the perfect time to start delegating and lengthening that rope!

HOW TO DELEGATE

Okay, let's be honest. The *how* is the part of delegating we leaders often screw up. We've come to see that our team members are thoroughbreds and they've got the capacity for more, but now it's our turn as leaders to step up and do the actual work of delegating *and* do it well.

Remember when I said that delegation is intentional? That it isn't a blind handoff but a step-by-step process? Here are the steps you can take to avoid screwing it up and frustrating yourself and your team members.

Take Inventory

First, you need to audit your work responsibilities. Think about all the things you do in a day, week, month, quarter, and year—from taking out the trash, to hiring, to annual planning. (To help you organize your thoughts, you can use the free Time Tracker worksheet at ramseysolutions.com/delegation.) List out all the tasks you do and put them in these four categories:

1. **Important**

   This is work you're good at and love. You might even call it your "sweet spot."

2. **Less Important**

   This is work you're good at but don't love. As you do these things, you're thinking, *Surely there's someone better built for this, right?*

3. **Time Waster**

   This is work you're bad at but like. You might find yourself asking, *Is it smart to keep doing this when others may be faster and better?*

4. **Hate It**

   This is work you're bad at and hate. These tasks suck the life out of you, *and* you suck at doing them.

Putting the work on paper like this will give you clarity. You'll likely see right away what you need to be spending more of your time on and what you need to get off your plate. (Hint: The tasks you need to delegate are in your Time Waster and Hate It categories.)

Create a KRA

Once you've determined what responsibilities and tasks you need to off-load, it's time to create a KRA. I introduced the idea of a KRA earlier in the book. It's essentially a one-page document that outlines the two to four Key Results Areas a team member is responsible for in their role. A KRA is not to be mistaken as a general job description. It's specific to the team member and how their work relates to the current business unit objectives. It includes a "What Winning Looks Like" and a "What It Will Take" section that describes specific goals and expectations of each Key Results Area. Depending on the objectives you're trying to meet, the details of these sections might change seasonally.

For example, maybe you've put accounting in your Hate It list of things to do. You're in good company—*a lot* of EntreLeaders I know really suck at accounting. This was me. I can do accounting, but I hate it, so this was one of the first things I delegated when I started hiring people. If this is you, you've probably been keeping the books for years—sort of. But carrying out that task probably looks like this: you put it off until the last possible moment every month, and then when you finally sit down to do it, you dread every minute of it like it was a high school term paper. Instead of prolonging the agony, you need to delegate this to a team member who enjoys and excels at this type of work.

To write a KRA for this accountant role, you would need to do the following:

1. **Write a one-sentence summary of the role.**
    "Summary" example: *Manage company's finances, preparing and examining financial records to ensure accuracy and compliance.*

2. **Determine two to four Key Results Areas that are high-level, evergreen responsibilities of the role.**
    "Key Results Area" examples: *Prepare quarterly budgets and complete tax preparation and payroll.*

3. **Write one sentence describing what winning looks like in each of these Key Results Areas.**

   "What Winning Looks Like" example: *Complete timely reconciliation of all company bank statements and bookkeeping ledgers.*

4. **Write two to four bullet points for each Key Results Area, describing the high-level expectations of what it will take to achieve success in each area.**

   "What It Will Take" example: *Initiate and manage new accounting software across all company divisions.*

Writing a KRA might seem tricky at first. (To give you a starting point, we've added a KRA template for you to use and reference at ramseysolutions.com/delegation.) But the exercise of writing a KRA is helpful because it makes you think through all aspects of the work and gives you a framework for the role that acts as a communication tool between you and the team member.

Once you identify the team member who can best fill the role (the next step in the process), you can later tailor the KRA together. You can discuss each "Key Results Area" and update the "What Winning Looks Like" and the "What It Will Take" sections based on the team member's unique skills and the unique needs of the business at that particular time.

Identify Ready Team Members

Your next move is to identify people in your organization who could take on the work you've pinpointed in the KRA. Remember, this isn't a time to feel guilty about dumping these things onto someone else. Delegating is *not* dumping. It's a time to help both you and your team members work in a more optimized way. What's a Time Waster or a Hate It task to you might be someone else's sweet spot and a way for them to grow in the company.

List your key team members and their current roles. Look over your list and note who's a natural fit to take over tasks you're ready to move off your plate. Keep in mind the essential qualities of *integrity* and *competency*. You want to give the right things to the right people. Ask yourself, *What are their skill sets? What are they good at? How could they grow? What's that person's current workload?* Be ready to remove things from their plate if you need to so they have room to tackle their new opportunities.

Sometimes during this process, you realize you've got people on your team who aren't carrying their weight. If that's the case, it's time for a hard conversation. Don't put this off. To be unclear is to be unkind, so handle it directly. Remember, you can't delegate to donkeys.

This process might also reveal that you don't currently have the right team members for the roles you need to delegate. In that case, the KRA you've identified will turn into your next hire. But if you're in a position where you just can't hire who you need quite yet, that's okay. You've still got your KRA identified and that will help you set goals and look at other options until you can hire a full-time team member.

Here are some effective options that could bridge the gap until you can make the hire:

- **Outsource the work to another company or person.** Competency and integrity still matter, so don't rush this. Dig into candidate backgrounds so you're sure they still fit your company's needs and values. This is nonnegotiable, no matter if it's temporary. And remember, thoroughbreds run with other thoroughbreds, so ask for recommendations from colleagues.

  With outsourcing, also be mindful to take a hard line on any roles related to money. The wrong person in a financial seat can destroy everything. Don't outsource these roles and allow people you don't know and trust to handle your money.
- **Automate the task.** Look for a software program or other technology to manage tasks from customer relationships to email marketing.
- **Delete the task entirely.** If the specific task is barely profitable and bogging down the team, stop and critique it. If it's complicated and causing major stress beyond its benefits, eliminate it altogether.

Take Time to Train Team Members

You've done the work to identify the KRA and the right team member. Now it's time to teach. For many leaders, this is the love-hate part of delegation. Let's face it—training isn't every leader's strong suit, *and* it takes extra time. Not all of us can be as epic as Mr. Miyagi in *The Karate Kid*, catching flies with chopsticks and creating poetic "wax on, wax off" teaching moments. But if you're not careful, this is the part where you can sabotage the process and easily slip back into thoughts like, *It's just easier and faster if I do it.* You need to remember why you're delegating in the first place. Taking time to train your team member properly now will increase your time and capacity later. It's one of the best investments you can make in yourself, your team, and your company.

Start by having a high-level conversation with the team member that introduces the new opportunity coming their way. Explain why the person was chosen for this role. Discuss how they're specifically qualified and how the role connects with their career journey and goals.

Next, outline the KRA you've identified for the role. This is where you get down in the weeds of what you need and expect. Define why the task is important. **If you don't clearly communicate your expectations, the job will never be completed to your satisfaction.**

Lastly, let them know you're committed to coaching them thoroughly and giving them the resources to win. Explain that there will be a handoff process over a certain amount of time that will include these three steps:

Step 1: *I do. You watch.*
This is a chance for the team member to observe you and ask questions. During this step, the rope is short with very little slack.

Step 2: *You do. I watch.*
This is a chance for the team member to do the hands-on work and receive direct feedback. During this step, the rope is extended a little further but is still fairly short.

Step 3: *You do. I check in.*

This is a chance for the team member to work more independently with regular check-ins along the way. During this step, the rope is lengthened but is still attached to the leader.

For example, let's say you're delegating a copywriting role. The team member might first have a one- to two-week period to study any company style guides, templates, and samples of things you've written, such as copy for company web pages, emails, and lead magnets. Then they begin to write copy themselves. During this phase, their work might be under review for ninety days with direct feedback and edits on every email, ad, or product description they write to make sure they're meeting your company's brand guidelines for voice and style. Once the team member has developed a pattern of fewer and fewer revisions, they can have more rope to write independently—but with established rhythms of accountability.

During this initial conversation and throughout the training, it's important to remind yourself and your team member that practice is vital to getting better. Be clear that you're a coach, not a cop, and that there's room for grace along the way. This creates space for mistakes and accountability, not micromanaging. You don't want your team member to float blindly, only to learn after the fact the result isn't what you wanted. You also don't want to make the hairs on the back of their neck stand up while you stand behind them barking out directions. Let them know your goal is to find the balance of trusting and giving them freedom but also coaching and guiding their growth.

This conversation is also a great time to reiterate the importance of being coachable. Let them know you expect them to be mature enough to know their limitations and ask for help. The process of delegation is easier and quicker if they're transparent and comfortable enough in their own skin to say, "Help me with this. I have no clue what this means. Why did we do it that way?" The process is slower or stalls out altogether if they fight the coaching, thinking their way is better or choosing to fake it till they make it.

Levels of Delegation

Training makes it possible to verify a team member's competency and best set them up for success. Depending on how complex the role is, there are different levels of training and delegation that need to happen. In his book *Principle-Centered Leadership*, Dr. Stephen R. Covey talks about these levels. He calls the most basic level of delegation "gofer delegation" and the highest level of delegation "stewardship delegation."

Gofer Delegation

Gofer delegation is usually for entry-level or temp positions. At the gofer level, team members are typically assigned simple tasks that can be easily verified and measured. These tasks include things like making copies, delivering packages, and running errands. You can hand these tasks off and *boom*—you can high-five that they're complete. Training people to take on gofer tasks gets you away from being the chief everything officer. You no longer have to be down in the weeds packing the product, figuring the postage, making the label, and doing the shipping yourself. You can teach someone else these basic tasks so you can work on the bigger deals. It eliminates frustration and helps you work more on your business, not in it.

Stewardship Delegation

Stewardship delegation is for more advanced positions like management. At this level, you're delegating concepts, not tasks. The stewardship rope is much longer than the gofer rope. You can trust the team member to reach the results you've agreed upon, but you're not as involved with all the details or the method they use to get there. It's basically delegating to a rock star who has a whole team of rock stars they can delegate to. You have confidence they'll steward the concepts and the results well. This is when you begin to really build a business that you run instead of the business running you. It's fully extending the rope but never letting go completely.

In business, the rope metaphor always stays in play. In parenting, you must let go of the rope eventually with your kids because they'll grow to be adults, move on, and stand on their own. But in business, the team you've built stays with you. They don't stand on their own; they stand *within* your company's culture. The rope needs to stay in place because you'll always need a way to monitor expectations. You can't *expect* what you don't *inspect*.

Accountability

For purposes of accountability, *all* levels of delegation demand some verification of performance. It doesn't matter if you're Warren Buffett; you've still got the end of the rope. As leader of Berkshire Hathaway, Warren buys profitable, autonomous companies with competent leadership, but he doesn't just turn his back and walk away. He still has a hold of the rope. It might be ten million miles long, but he and his leadership team have the rope and are still looking at performance metrics.

As a delegating leader, you'll always at some level inspect what you expect. Your team could be in another division, another state, or a multibillion-dollar operation with lots of profit centers around the world, but there's still an inspection level and an expectation level. It doesn't matter how long the rope is—you've still got a hold of the end of it.

Authority

But holding on to the rope doesn't mean you don't give a team member authority to do the job you've asked them to do. The worst thing you can do as a leader is go through all the work of auditing your responsibilities, identifying the right team member to delegate to, creating a specific KRA for them, training them for months and months, and then not give them authority. Delegation doesn't work *at all* without authority to act.

Giving people responsibility for things they don't have the authority to act on puts them in a frustrating, horrible position. It would be like me saying, "Hey, VP, I want you to run a huge live event, but I'll still need to approve any expense over $50." That would be paralyzing to him, his team, and the process. He'd be coming to me, asking for permission for every little thing. The event would never get off the ground! That's micromanaging at its worst, and it doesn't serve anyone well. In fact, it undermines business and relationships.

Ronald Reagan said, "Surround yourself with the best people you can find, delegate authority, and don't interfere." If a team member has enough integrity and competency for you to delegate to them in the first place, then you need to get out of their way and give them room to do the job. Yes, hold them accountable for the work. But give them full authority to do the work.

When I got into business thirty years ago, bankers were respected in the community—because they did actual banking. In those days, the branch manager in most banks, including the bank I dealt with, had a $100,000 lending authority. He had business acumen and could loan $100,000 without asking anybody. The average big-bank branch manager now can only loan about $2,000 without permission. They can't even waive your overdraft fees without asking their regional manager. Branch managers have become no more than glorified tellers!

The banking industry is a classic case of big responsibility, little authority. Sure, branch managers have the title and the corner office, but not a lot of money to back it up. It's a frustrating shell of a position. They're held accountable for creating relationships in the marketplace and for creating loan production, but they're not allowed to produce loans without strings attached and without all the central-office garbage that's involved.

And so, surprise—the industry is failing as a result. It's falling in on itself because it's lost its soul in dealing with its key people. And guess what? The good old bankers left, started small community banks, and got rich. I have about six to eight friends who used to be branch managers but moved on to make millions starting community banks. They knew how to do banking—how to build relationships, how to be there for businesses, how to serve people—rather than look at every customer as a transaction unit.

In other words, titles and money don't make a leader. They're hollow. If you give someone a title but don't give them the power and authority to go with it, it's a joke and everybody knows it.

Mastering the Rope

You know you've mastered the rope and reached the highest level of delegation when you as the leader delegate leadership. Once you get to this stage, you're delegating concepts to people who are in turn delegating gofer details to even more people. That's when you know you've got a complete and effective delegation process in place. Of course, the layers of delegation grow deeper the more team members you have. But regardless of how many layers deep your team goes, the goal is that you've created enough margin for yourself to work only on high-level concepts, not all the intricate details. Mastering the delegation rope means you're now able to work *on* your business, not just *in* your business.

As the leader of Ramsey Solutions for thirty years, I'm at a point where I only get involved in two things: new things and broken things. I've fully delegated all the operational things. Sure, I'm holding the end of the rope, following the metrics, reading high points, and doing random checks to keep my finger on the pulse of what's going on, but I spend very little time on areas that are working. My time is best spent focusing on high-level areas of concern or on new and unproven areas led by new and unproven leaders.

What about you? After learning what delegation is and when and how to implement it, how will you more strategically focus your time and apply delegation to move your business forward?

As you think about your answer to that question, I want to give you a framework to consider. But first, I want to take you back where we began. Remember? You were running what seemed like a never-ending race.

DELEGATION APPLIED

Before you picked up this book, it's safe to say that at some point as a small-business owner, you've felt like the odds were stacked against you. Even as you have run mile after monotonous mile on the business-startup treadmill, even as the mechanical belt under your feet has turned and turned, somehow, you haven't gained much distance or momentum. Instead, you only seemed to max out your time, energy, and resources.

The sad fact is, the odds *are* stacked against you. For every business that opens, roughly one business shuts down.[4] That trend has held true year after year—in good and bad economic conditions. It's no surprise, then, at some point you would feel discouraged, even disconnected, from the dream that got you started in the first place.

The truth is, you can run and run and run, but alone, you'll only go as far as your education, ability, character, capacity, and vision can take you. My friend and leadership expert John Maxwell calls this "The Leadership Lid." But here's the good news: *you* are in control of the treadmill. At any time, *you* can take control of the race by hitting the red STOP button on the treadmill dashboard. *You* can choose to get off that human hamster wheel, pick up a rope, start delegating, and get on a new path forward.

At Ramsey, we've identified this as the pivotal point between the Treadmill Operator and the Pathfinder Stages of Business, the first two of five stages in the EntreLeadership Framework. Delegation—everything you've learned in this book—is the strategic bridge between the two. In fact, as you continue to grow your company through all five Stages of Business, you'll find that delegation never stops. At every stage of growth, it will be central to your success. Let's take a look and see how delegation is applied in each stage.

The EntreLeadership Framework: Five Stages of Business

Stage One: Treadmill Operator

The Treadmill Operator is the first of the five Stages of Business. At this stage, you can feel like the whole freaking thing is riding on you. And even though it's hard, the do-whatever-it-takes nature of this stage definitely has value and serves a purpose. It's an exhilarating and an exhausting season, but that's exactly what it should be—a season. This isn't a stage you want to camp out in forever, because honestly, it will wear you out and eventually take you down. If you want to lead a business that thrives, you can't just own a *job*. You have to stop letting your business run you and start running your business with your goals in mind. This is where delegation comes in. Identifying and training others to help carry the load at this stage will be key in moving to the more strategic Pathfinder stage.

Stage Two: Pathfinder

In the Pathfinder stage, you're struggling to have a clear vision and direction forward. The goal in this stage is to create time to work *on* your business—not just *in* it. In this stage, you need to stop spending 100 percent of your time focusing on tasks and start making space to focus on yourself as a leader and on your strategy for your business. The only way to do this well is through delegation. Delegation will be critical to growing your capacity so you can expand your footprint and serve more people.

Stage Three: Trailblazer

In the Trailblazer stage, you're striving to establish plans and processes to scale your business. You're working to get the fundamentals of a high-powered and healthy organization in place—like core values, long-term goals, and a meaningful mission—so you get consistent results. But you need a strong team and a winning strategy to rise to the top of your industry. Again, delegation will continue to play a huge role here. You'll need to get your team to optimize and own their roles with excellence to achieve substantial growth and even greater results.

Stage Four: Peak Performer

In this stage, your challenge is being too comfortable. You as the owner need to continue to stretch yourself to sustain success, vigilantly guard the culture you've grown, and set your business up for

DAVE RAMSEY

the long run. The good news is, you're not alone. At this point, the entire company is helping you move the business forward. You're all thinking about how to serve people, grow profits, and take performance to the next level. Delegation comes into play in a big way as you empower a deep bench of leaders to carry out the mission, vision, and strategy of the business. Your focus will be on sustaining success and setting your business up for the long run.

Stage Five: Legacy Builder

When you reach the Legacy Builder stage, you have a lot to be proud of! At this stage, you're creating a succession plan and preparing for transition. This is where all your strategic delegation will show its best fruit as your team will keep the company in good hands when you step down. The goal is for them to carry on the work you started with just as much drive, passion, and energy as you've had all along. This is the ultimate delegation!

After seeing how delegation relates to all five Stages of Business, maybe it's inspired you to see how you can successfully lengthen the rope in your current stage. So let's go back to the question I posed earlier: After learning what delegation is and when and how to implement it, how will you more strategically focus your time and apply delegation to move your business forward?

Remember, your business will only grow and thrive to the extent that you will commit to delegating and mastering the rope. It's how you'll confidently build and scale. It's how you'll grow quality team members full of integrity and competency. It's how you and your team will win.

CONCLUSION

Thirty years ago, I set out to live the American Dream of owning and operating my own business. At age twenty-six, I had over four million dollars in real estate with a net worth of over one million dollars. However, I had built my business with too much debt. When my primary lender was sold to another bank, all my notes were called all at once. I spent the next two and a half years losing everything I owned. I was sued, foreclosed on, and finally went bankrupt. I was broke and broken, with a new baby, a toddler, and a marriage hanging on by a thread.

I started over, teaching people to handle money, running our little business from a card table in our living room. But this time my approach was different. I was still a go-getter, but I made a deliberate decision to operate my life and my business by Christian principles, not my own. I'm convinced it's the reason we've had the success we have today.

When I maxed out all the hours of my day with one-on-one financial counseling and speaking engagements, I hired my first team member to help carry the counseling load. Then I hired my second team member to be our secretary, bookkeeper, and reception-ist (and everything else that needed to be done). We put our heads down and worked long hours. When we looked up a year or so later, we had seven people on the team and had graduated to a bigger, better office. It was at this point that I realized the need to develop my team members so they could help me lead. The thought terrified me.

I was a young entrepreneur, confident in my own ability to get things done. But I was really unsure about giving up control and letting someone else lead. Before I knew it, though, we had formed three departments within the company, and I began the slow and thorough process of pouring hours and hours into the three men who would lead those departments. My goal was to teach them to know what I would do at any given time in any situation. This was the first time I intentionally put delegation into practice. It worked. They became some of my most trusted advisors.

With our team now at around two hundred leaders and over a thousand team members serving millions of customers and generating hundreds of millions of dollars in revenues, it's truly amazing to think about our humble beginnings and all we've done to develop our delegation process throughout the company.

Just recently, we went through a major delegation moment at the Legacy Builder stage. We transitioned *The Dave Ramsey Show* to *The Ramsey Show* so other Ramsey Personalities could be show hosts. I'm 100 percent behind this move, and it's the right thing to do for the future of our company. But I'll be honest. When I finally saw the new studio set with the new name and someone else sitting behind the desk, I seriously felt the earth move under my feet. Of all the delegation I've done through the years, this took releasing control and lengthening the rope to another level! But it will undoubtedly take our company to another level too. That's the reward of delegation.

Whether you're sitting at your card table, running on your treadmill, blazing trails, or making room for others to sit behind your desk, mastering the rope is not easy. It shouldn't be. There's too much at stake, and there are people involved.

But I promise you, it's unbelievably worth it.

NOTES

1. "Gary Player," Britannica, last updated October 28, 2022, https://www.britannica.com/biography/Gary-Player.

2. Guy Yocom, "My Shot: Gary Player," Golf Digest, last updated August 12, 2010, https://www.golfdigest.com/story/myshot_gd0210.

3. Pam Windsor, "Michael W. Smith Reflects on the Power of a Song—35 No. 1 Hits Later," Forbes, April 20, 2019, https://www.forbes.com/sites/pamwindsor/2019/04/30/michael-w-smith-reflects-on-the-power-of-song-35-no-1-hits-later/?sh=37f374d82545.

4. "Frequently Asked Questions," U.S. Small Business Administration Office of Advocacy, September 2019, https://cdn.advocacy.sba.gov/wp-content/uploads/2019/09/24153946/Frequently-Asked-Questions-Small-Business-2019-1.pdf.

ABOUT THE AUTHOR

 Dave Ramsey is America's trusted voice on money and business. He's a #1 National bestselling author and host of *The Ramsey Show*, heard by more than 18 million listeners each week. Dave's eight national bestselling books include *The Total Money Makeover, Baby Steps Millionaires,* and *EntreLeadership.* Since 1992, Dave has helped people take control of their money, build wealth, and enhance their lives. He also serves as CEO of Ramsey Solutions.

RESOURCES

To get all these resources and more, go to
ramseysolutions.com/delegation

12 Components to a Good Hire Article

Learn the process we follow at Ramsey Solutions when looking to hire a new team member so you can get the right people in the right seats on the bus.

Time Tracker Worksheet

Track your responsibilities for a week to learn what is important for you to focus on and what can be delegated to someone else.

KRA Template

Document what winning looks like for you and your team with this editable template. Summarize a role and create key results areas so you always have clarity in your team member's roles.

EntreLeadership Elite

A membership to help you lead your team and grow your business the Ramsey way.